IMAGES
of Aviation

LUFTHANSA

How it all began. On 6 January 1919, Deutsche Luft-Reederei, the world's first airline, opened scheduled airmail services on the Berlin-Weimar route. The following month services from Berlin to Hamburg and the Ruhr also began. Here airmail – apparently mostly newspapers – is delivered to the Gelsenkirchen post office.

Cover picture: The Junkers-Ju 52/3m is synonymous with Lufthansa and it is appropriate that the airline continues to operate one on pleasure flights through its Historical Foundation. Built in 1935, it joined Lufthansa as D-AQUI *Fritz Simon*. Later used on floats by DNL, it returned to Lufthansa, but went to Norway after the war. After a long history in Ecuador and the USA, it was purchased by Lufthansa for $200,000, flown in a Boeing 747 to Hamburg and restored, flying again in April 1986. Although marked as D-AQUI, its genuine registration, worn beneath the tailplane, is D-CDLH.

IMAGES
of Aviation

LUFTHANSA

Compiled by
Mike Hooks

TEMPUS

First published 1999
Copyright © Mike Hooks, 1999

Tempus Publishing Limited
The Mill, Brimscombe Port,
Stroud, Gloucestershire, GL5 2QG

ISBN 0 7524 1702 9

Typesetting and origination by
Tempus Publishing Limited
Printed in Great Britain by
Midway Clark Printing, Wiltshire

In contrast to the picture on p.2, these days Lufthansa uses somewhat larger aircraft! Here, a Boeing 747 freighter is loaded through the nose with international standard containers by means of a special cargo loader.

Contents

A passenger boards L.V.G. C.VI D 34 of Deutsche Luft-Reederei at Berlin-Johannisthal via a simple step-ladder. Judging by the passenger's apparel, it was going to be a cold flight in the open-cockpit biplane!

Introduction

German civil aviation following the First World War began on 8 January 1919 when the Reich Aviation Office granted a licence to the new Deutsche Luft-Reederei (DLR) to operate civilian services. On 5 February converted military aircraft began to fly mail between Berlin and Weimar. Wartime military mail services had provided useful experience and post-war successful operations led to DLR becoming a founder member of the International Air Traffic Association when it was established in The Hague on 28 August 1919. The following year, DLR linked with KLM of Holland and DDL of Denmark to open the first international route from Malmö-Copenhagen via Warnemünde, Hamburg, Bremen, to Amsterdam.

Air transport was beginning to grow, and in Germany a number of small companies sprang up thanks to financial support from the government. Among these were the Lloyd Luftverkehr Sablatnig, founded by the North German Lloyd shipping line and the Sablatnig Aircraft Works in 1920, forerunner of the Lloyd Luftdienst GmbH. In 1921 a more complex grouping took place. The groups involved in DLR – AEG, Hapag and Luftschiffbau Zeppelin – formed Aero-Union, a holding company, in April, while, in November, another Berlin-based airline was established, Deutsche Russische-Verkehrs GmbH (Deruluft), owned jointly by DLR and represented by Aero-Union. Deruluft began services on 1 May 1922 between Königsberg and Moscow.

On 6 February 1923, DLR and the Lloyd Luftdienst group merged their inventories of aircraft, spares, operations and facilities into two companies, Deutscher Aero-Lloyd and Junkers Luftverkehr, the latter being an operating branch of the aircraft manufacturer. These two companies continued to grow but, by 1926, the government, concerned at the financial support it was giving, insisted on amalgamation, and on 6 January 1926 Deutsche Lufthansa was founded.

More than 600 A.E.G. J.1 two-seat armoured reconnaissance aircraft, powered by a 200hp Benz engine, were built after the 1918 armistice, according to the Inter Allied Commission. They were used for a number of tasks, and C4871 shows a hastily applied Deutsche Flugpost titling.

Like the A.E.G. J.1, the L.V.G. C.VI two-seater had a 200hp Benz IV engine. Around 1,000 of these aircraft were built. Loading mail at Gelsenkirchen has attracted an interested crowd. Oddly, this banner says Deutsche Luftpost. Deutsche Luft-Reederei opened scheduled airmail services on 5 February 1919 between Berlin and Weimar.

A smart A.E.G. N.1 of Deutsche Luft-Reederei – some spellings show the hyphen, while others are like this. Powered by a 200hp Benz IV, the N.1 had a small cabin for passengers with the pilot above and behind. A certain number were on the German civil register in 1919; D 38 subsequently passed to Lufthansa on its formation in 1926, but was retired two years later.

No scheduled services were operated during the winter, but commercial flights began on 6 April and, by the end of the year, nearly four million miles had been flown. Among the routes was the first night passenger service between Berlin and Königsberg which connected with Deruluft's Moscow service, enabling Moscow to Berlin to be flown in one day.

In April 1926, the first month of operations, Lufthansa carried 6,940kg of freight, while in April 1927 it had increased to 33,809kg – up 500%. The airline had forecast that 'air freight is likely to develop into an important, if not the most important, revenue earner in air transport' and was well on the way to proving it. By 1928 supplementary special freight flights were being operated from Berlin to London and Paris, while Junkers engineers were converting the first freight-only aircraft, the single-engine Ju 52/1m, which could carry a 2,000kg payload for 1,000km.

With the arrival of the Junkers-G 24, Lufthansa's first tri-motor aircraft, routes to the Far East were explored. On 23 July 1926 three G 24s left Berlin for Peking, overflying Russia, and arriving on 30 August. By the end of that year, Lufthansa was operating 120 aircraft of various types.

The airline was in the forefront of technical development in blind flying, navigation, radio and air traffic control – beacon-lit routes for night flying were supplemented by thirteen ground radio transmitters – and was using advanced aircraft types. The robust single-engined Junkers-F13, a mainstay of early operations, was reliable and strong with its corrugated skin, a feature which was to follow on later Junkers up to the Ju 52/3m. This tri-motor airliner, which was to epitomize Lufthansa in the 1930s, went on to become the Luftwaffe's main transport aircraft. It is with great pride that Lufthansa still operates a 1930s-built Ju 52/3m on pleasure flying to this day.

The possible wish of passengers to sleep during their flight was initially solved by Lufthansa in 1927 with the twin-engined Albatros L 73 biplane, whose eight seats could be converted into four bunks for night flights. The following year, those who wished to eat during their flight were catered for in three fifteen-passenger Junkers-G 31s flying from Berlin to other European cities.

Lufthansa and its forerunners had long been interested in forming links with South America and the first of these came in 1919 when German participation helped in the formation of the Sociedad Colombo Alemana de Transportes Aéreos (SCADTA) at Baranquilla, Colombia. The airline bought two Junkers-F 13 floatplanes and employed German pilots, beginning regular services in 1921.

Built as a long-range bomber, the Friedrichshafen G.IIIA served from early 1917 to the armistice, and 338 were built by HFW and Daimler, with two 260hp Mercedes D.IVA engines. Deutsche Luft-Reederei acquired D 121 from Lloyd L.V. Sablatnig in November 1919 to fly mail between Berlin and other cities during a railway strike.

9

A number of A.E.G. J.IIs were modified by Deutsche Luft-Reederei to have an enclosed two-seat cabin, with the pilot in an open cockpit. This unmarked example was to become D 23 and had a 200hp Benz IV engine.

In 1924 Deutscher Aero-Lloyd and SCADTA established the Condor Syndikat in Berlin to study the viability of an inter-American network between Colombia, Central America and the USA, also looking at the possibility of a transatlantic service to South America. They bought two Dornier Wal flying-boats, *Atlantico* and *Pacifico*, and carried out trial flights to Key West and Miami. Political problems, however, ended the experiment.

In January 1927 Lufthansa founded the Syndicato Condor Ltda in Rio de Janeiro as a Brazilian airline, while the following year a Junkers-G 24 floatplane visited cities to be included in the Condor network.

On 22 July 1929 a Heinkel He 12 floatplane catapulted from the passenger liner *Bremen* 400km from New York took the first airmail to New York and, on the return journey, the Heinkel was catapulted 8km west of Cherbourg to fly the 800km to Bremerhaven where a connecting flight took the mail from America onwards to Berlin. These Lufthansa services were expanded during the following three years.

In May 1930 a close co-operation between Lufthansa, Condor and Hapag led to the airship *Graf Zeppelin* making its first journey from Friedrichshafen to South America, reducing the journey time from Berlin to Rio to five days. A further excursion came in November 1931 when the twelve-engined Dornier Do X flying-boat with Lufthansa and Condor backing flew 33,650km in 198 flying hours on a South and North American trip, making a number of demonstration flights. South Atlantic services continued with connecting flights to steamers carrying mail. For the *Graf Zeppelin*, Lufthansa flew mail to Friedrichshafen for onward flight to Condor in South America, which distributed it.

Further Zeppelin crossings in 1932 were followed by Lufthansa's charter of the steamer *Westfalen* from Norddeutscher Lloyd for conversion into a floating stop-over for Dornier Wals on the South Atlantic service. It was fitted with a Heinkel-developed catapult and a crane at the stern to recover flying-boats.

On 29 May 1933 the first catapult take-off by a Wal was made at Bremerhaven, while on 6 June the Wal *Monsun* undertook the first catapulted flight to Natal. The first scheduled flight from Germany to South America – which was also the first scheduled trans-ocean flight in the world – took place on 3 February 1934. The Wal took four to five days to cover the 11,369km from Berlin via Stuttgart, Seville, Bathurst and Natal to Rio. With the success of the *Westfalen* and the upgrading of the service from fortnightly to weekly, Lufthansa introduced the ten-tonne Wal – the former weighed eight tonnes – and commissioned a second catapult ship, the *Schwabenland*. The latter was at the mouth of the Gambia river, while the *Westfalen* was cruising off the Brazilian mainland near the island of Fernando Noronha.

A night service was introduced in 1935, further reducing the flying time between Germany and Buenos Aires to three and a half days. In that year Lufthansa took a substantial stake in the new Deutsche Zeppelinreederei (DZR) and, on 25 August, the 100th scheduled airmail flight across the Atlantic took place, marking some four million letters carried. The volume continued to grow and Lufthansa ordered a third support ship, the *Ostmark*, faster and smaller than its predecessors.

On 26 April 1937 the *Graf Zeppelin* began its last scheduled flight. In 1936 it had carried 572 passengers between Europe and South America. A new company, Sociedad Ecuatoriana de Transportes Aéreos (SEDTA) was founded in July, beginning operations with two Junkers-W 34s chartered from Lufthansa the following spring; Lufthansa eventually took over as major shareholder. Further South American expansion involved the setting up of another company in Peru, the last operation by Lufthansa outside Europe.

Tests using two Blohm und Voss Ha 139 four-engined seaplanes took place between August and November 1937 using two floating depots, *Schwabenland* and *Friesenland* and involving catapult take-offs, the first being from the Azores to New York. These continued into the following year when, on 10-11 August, Lufthansa's Focke-Wulf Fw 200 Condor D-ACON, fitted with extra fuel tanks, flew from Berlin-Staaken to New York's Floyd Bennett Field in twenty-four hours and thirty-six minutes, averaging 255km/h. The non-stop flight was via Hamburg, Glasgow, Newfoundland and Halifax. It was to be another eighteen years before Lufthansa operated its next scheduled North Atlantic flight.

Aero Lloyd's much modified A.E.G. J.II (K) D 9 of 1918 contrasts with the previous picture. Powered by a 200hp BMW IV which gave a cleaner appearance, D 9 was destroyed in October 1923. The (K) designation indicated *kabine*.

Some 1,000 L.V.G. C.VIs were built at Berlin-Johannisthal for reconnaissance, all with 200hp Benz engines. Locally-based Luft Lloyd's D 89 had a rudimentary partial enclosure with side windows for the two-seat rear cockpit.

Lloyd-Luftverkehr Sablatnig, founded in 1919 by Norddeutscher Lloyd Sablatnig Flugzeugbau, opened a Berlin-Stralsund service with the six-passenger Sablatnig P.III. Powered by various engines, this is probably the first aircraft, D 2, with a 240hp Armstong Siddeley Puma. Later owned by Lufthansa, it was dismantled in March 1932.

Lufthansa began serving Chile with its own aircraft in 1938 on the Buenos Aires-Santiago de Chile route; service to Brazil followed. By January 1939 the airline demonstrated a level of performance not approached by any other – a 15,039km route from Berlin to Santiago de Chile.

In 1939 an earthquake in Chile took the second four-engined Dornier Do 26 flying-boat *Seefalke* from Wärnemunde to Rio with 567kg of medical supplies, covering a distance of 10,700km in thirty-six hours. In June that year the first of two Focke-Wulf Condors for Condor – an appropriate coincidence – was delivered across the South Atlantic, taking nine hours and forty-seven minutes for the Bathurst to Natal flight.

As well as spreading west, Lufthansa was looking east and in 1930 concluded a ten-year agreement with China for an airmail service. The Eurasia Aviation Corporation, based in Nanking, was one-third owned by Lufthansa who supplied the aircraft, Junkers-F 13s and W 33s, plus crews and spares.

New routes were developed and Ju 52/3ms were delivered to China; by 1938 Afghanistan was in the network. Another milestone came in November that year when a Condor flew 14,278km from Berlin to Tokyo. An air traffic agreement with Japan extended Lufthansa's existing Berlin-Bangkok service to Tokyo, the proving flight being made by Ju 52/3m D-AGAK in 1939. However, the outbreak of war in Europe killed the route.

In 1938, the last complete pre-war year flown, Lufthansa carried 287,000 passengers, flying more than 15 million miles, making 52,619 domestic flights within Germany and 13,483 international. Berlin-Tempelhof was the origination airport for twenty-one routes. In 1940 the Chinese suspended Eurasia service and German personnel left China.

The outbreak of war put an end to the vast majority of Lufthansa operations, although a few scheduled services were flown. A famous photograph of Lisbon Airport showed Lufthansa and British DC-3s side-by-side on the tarmac.

One of the older biplanes which soldiered on for some years with various airlines was the L.V.G. C.V and Lufthansa had D-1179 *Bisam* in 1926-1927. It was burned in August the following year. At least two of this happy group appear to be going flying!

L.F.G. V-130 Stresa-land D 796 in the markings of Luftverkehr Pomern and with the useful load of 700kg marked on the fuselage, later served with Lufthansa as *Stettin*. It was powered at various times with a Benz IV, Ju L2 or BMW IV engine and was last recorded in August 1931 with E. Klutke, Berlin. Lufthansa had used it to serve seaside resorts.

Following the annexation of Austria in 1938, Lufthansa had taken over the routes and equipment of the country's airline, Oesterreichische Luftverkehrs AG. In 1943, after the occupation of France, some routes and equipment of Air France were also absorbed.

On 21 April 1945 the last scheduled service of the original Lufthansa left Berlin for Munich and Madrid, operated by Condor D-ASHH *Hessen*. It never arrived, being shot down by Allied forces at Piesenkofen, Germany. Another ten years were to pass before the post-war Lufthansa operated its first service.

Following several years of planning, the new Lufthansa was founded on 6 January 1953, based in Cologne. Four Super Constellations were ordered and the first regular pilot and navigator re-training courses began. A long-term contract with Hamburg Airport made a large hangar available as maintenance centre and the following year Luftag, as the new company had originally been christened, changed its name to Deutsche Lufthansa AG. Practical pilot training began at Hamburg in the winter of 1954-1955 on Saab Safirs and was followed by IFR instruction on DC-3s registered outside Germany.

In addition to the Super Constellation order, Lufthansa had contracted for four other new aircraft, Convair 340s, and the first arrived at Hamburg on 29 November 1954. Trial flights began on 1 March 1955 with British pilots and German co-pilots. The Paris Treaty restoring German sovereignty did not come into effect until May 5, but the Western Allies had granted Lufthansa special dispensation to begin flights that year. Initially they could not have all-German crews, but this was soon to change.

On 1 April 1955 scheduled domestic services began between Hamburg, Dusseldorf, Cologne, Frankfurt and Munich. In mid-April the first Super Constellation landed at Hamburg after a non-stop thirteen hours and forty-seven minutes flight from New York. TWA provided the pilots for initial services but, by March 1956, the first Super Constellation with an exclusively German crew left for the USA.

Three DC-3s had been acquired for domestic services the previous year which had also seen the formation of Deutsche Flugdienst by Norddeutscher Lloyd, Hamburg-America Line, German

National Railways and Lufthansa. This was soon to become Condor, Lufthansa's charter airline. New services opened with increasing rapidity and, by October 1956, Lufthansa had made its 1,000th scheduled North American flight. Five Convair 440s were bought in 1957 and were followed by others plus four L.1649 Starliners, the last derivative of the Constellation family, which were capable of flying non-stop from Germany to the USA with a full payload even against strong headwinds.

A new era began in 1958 when four Viscount 814s were ordered for European routes, Lufthansa's first experience of turboprop operations. The Viscount's big windows and seats, coupled with an almost total lack of vibration, made it very popular with passengers.

Meanwhile, the airline had opened its own flying school on 1 May 1956 at Bremen for basic training and refresher courses. Its first two aircraft were Beech Twin Bonanzas, ferried from Wichita, Kansas by German crews in December under very bad weather conditions. The Bremen school subsequently operated a number of other types including de Havilland Chipmunks and Saab Safirs for basic training. Later, training was undertaken at a Lufthansa Commercial Pilot's School set up at Phoenix, Arizona, where pilots flew the Great Lakes biplane, Beech Bonanza and Baron. After 225 hours in singles and twins, trainee pilots completed their basic training under European conditions with twenty-five hours on the Beech King Air fitted with instrumentation similar to that of the Boeing 737 to which they would then be posted. The latest Bremen equipment is the Piper Cheyenne.

Lufthansa entered the pure-jet age with the Boeing 707-430, an intercontinental jet which began service with the airline in 1960, opening more new routes to the Far East. With the requirement for jet equipment for European and Near East routes, Lufthansa ordered twenty-one Boeing 727s, the first of which arrived in early 1964. To cope with increasing freight demands, two 727-30s in the Quick-Change version were ordered.

The end of another era came in 1967 when the last Super Constellation was retired. The type had flown 83 million km for a total of 185,000 flight hours, equivalent to 108 times the distance from the Earth to the Moon.

Following participation at design stage in the development of the Boeing 737 short-haul jet, Lufthansa ordered twenty-one and the first ones off the production line were delivered to Germany

Another of Luftverkehr Pomern's L.F.G. V-130s used by Lufthansa in the 1920s was D 810. Of wooden construction with fabric covering, the V-130 had an enclosed four-passenger cabin with the pilot in an open cockpit above and forward of the cabin. D 810 was sold in 1930 to W. Przibilla, Breslau.

The Caspar C 35 Priwall was a one-off design to a Lufthansa specification. The enclosed passenger cabin had eight seats, while the two-crew cockpit was also enclosed. Of mainly wooden construction, it had a 500hp BMW VI engine and was named *Rostock*. Cargo services were also operated in 1928-1929 but the Caspar was destroyed in July 1930.

from February 1968. Another first came in March 1970 when Lufthansa became the first European airline to take delivery of a Boeing 747. In the same year the Douglas DC-10, another wide-body type, was ordered for delivery in 1973, while in 1971 the last turboprop, a Viscount, was retired. It is retained at Frankfurt for cabin training. By the end of 1971 the Lufthansa fleet consisted of seventy-five Boeing 707s, 727s, 737s and 747s.

Fifty years after the foundation of the pre-war Lufthansa in 1926, the company took delivery of its first Airbus A300 and this was the beginning of a long and beneficial relationship with the European manufacturer as various new types of Airbus were introduced over the years – the A310, A320, A321, A340 and A319. By mid-1998 the airline's fleet stood at thirteen A300s, nine A310s, thirty-three A320s, twenty A321s, fifteen A319s, seventeen A340s, eighteen Avro RJ85s, seventy-five Boeing 737s, forty-three Boeing 747s and thirty-two Canadair RJs. The Avro and Canadair RJs are operated by Lufthansa Cityline, previously DLT until it was taken over by Lufthansa. Included in the above totals are eleven Boeing 747s operated by Lufthansa Cargo Services, formerly German Cargo Services, which in 1998 bought five Boeing (formerly McDonnell Douglas) MD-11Fs.

The Condor fleet should also be mentioned, the Lufthansa charter subsidiary founded in 1955, which at mid-1998 stood at three Airbus A320s, four Boeing 737s, eighteen Boeing 757s, nine Boeing 767s and three McDonnell Douglas DC-10s.

This has been a very brief look at the history of Lufthansa through its aircraft, since this book is intended to be pictorial rather than comprehensive. To do justice to the airline would take a very thick book. Most of the information contained in this book came from the 1985 publication *The Lufthansa Story*, an excellent example of an in-house company history. Note that I have adopted the title Lufthansa throughout rather than constantly changing from Deutsche Lufthansa to Luft Hansa and so on.

Finally, my sincere thanks to the Lufthansa archive at Cologne for the supply of the great majority of the photographs used; their speedy response to my request for assistance was very much appreciated.

One
Lufthansa is Founded

With the foundation of Deutsche Lufthansa on 6 January 1926, the German airline scene became much stronger. Now the main operators, previously fragmented and with a variety of aircraft types, became a cohesive whole. Of course, there were problems, particularly with regard to standardizing on aircraft, but with its new strength Lufthansa was able to retire many of the older types, conversions from wartime aircraft which had never been particularly reliable or economic. There was also the question of spares: no company wants a disparate fleet requiring an enormous and complex spares holding. This was another area where economies could be made.

Since Junkers Luftverkehr was one of the companies involved in the 1926 amalgamation, it was not surprising that Lufthansa chose their F 13, first flown in June 1919, to replace a lot of the wartime conversions. A very advanced design, it was of all-metal construction with an enclosed four-passenger cabin and production aircraft had a 185hp BMW engine. Its corrugated Duralumin skin became a Junkers trademark for passenger-carrying aircraft right through to the Ju 52/3m. The F 13 could be operated on wheels, skis or floats and served with a number of airlines in the early days, earning a reputation for reliability and toughness.

Lufthansa continued its loyalty to Junkers right through to the four-engined Ju 90 of 1938, but of course bought other types as well.

Lufthansa inherited this Albatros L 58A in 1926 on its formation. The cantilever monoplane had a 360hp Rolls-Royce Eagle engine and seating for six passengers. Named *Wolkensegler*, D 576 was destroyed in a crash in Germany in June 1928.

Lufthansa ordered two Albatros L 73s, D 960 *Preussen* and D 961 *Brandenburg* which were delivered in 1926. Three different engine types were fitted at various times between 260 and 340hp, the last being the BMW VA which changed the designation to L 73C.

The Albatros L 73 could carry eight passengers, but was ordered for night flights, and during these the seats could be reclined as shown – hardly the epitome of comfort! The cabin appears to have the barest of essentials.

Sablatnig P III D 451 *Fliege* was one of about ten operated by Lufthansa from 1926, powered by a variety of engines. This one originally had a 240hp Armstrong Siddeley Puma, later changed to a 230hp Junkers L 2. It was dismantled in March 1932. Comparison with the picture on p.12 shows a redesign of the struts.

Seen at Stuttgart-Boblingen Airport alongside an Ad Astra Dornier Merkur, Lufthansa's Sablatnig PIII D 581 was named *Libelle*. The PIII could carry six passengers in an enclosed cabin, while the pilot was above and behind in an open cockpit. Like D 451, this was dismantled in March 1932.

Lufthansa took over nineteen Fokker F.IIs in 1926, all of which had been built in Germany and designated Fokker-Grulich F.II. Wings were built by Albatros, while fuselage construction and assembly was by Deutscher Aero Lloyd at Berlin-Staaken. Dr Ing Karl Grulich was responsible for the modifications. D 756 *Dievenow* had a BMW IV engine.

Fokker-Grulich F.II D 717, later named *Weichsel*, displays its strangely-shaped cargo door – the adjacent three-wheeled Phanomobil milk van is even stranger! This F.II survived to become D-OVAZ when the German registration system changed to letters instead of numbers.

The pilot of a Fokker-Grulich F.II looks on from the cockpit, a passenger remembers something he wants from his suitcase and some fairly chaotic loading goes on from a van and luggage cart!

A Lufthansa air-boy carried luggage to the aircraft and helped passengers to board via simple 'air-stairs'! The notice on the door of this Fokker-Grulich F.II reminds passengers not to open the door while the engine is running. Five passengers could be carried, including one alongside the pilot – no guessing who is going to sit there on this flight!

This view of Fokker-Grulich F.II *Werra* at last shows the beginnings of the use of a hyphen in the registration. Notable is the very small rudder and absence of fin. Originally fitted with a BMW IV engine, D-786 was later upgraded to F.IIB standard with a BMW V and, in 1934, was re-registered D-OGOT. It crashed in Germany on 24 July 1934.

To accommodate five passengers in a wider cabin, Fokker produced the F.III in 1921. Among the first deliveries was Dz 8 for Deutsche Luft-Reederei, (the registration applied to the Free State of Danzig). Powered by a BMW IV engine, Dz 8 subsequently became D 180 *Fürth* of Lufthansa but was lost in a crash near Heroldsbach, Germany on 6 September 1928 with three fatalities.

Deutsche Luft-Reederei began building Fokker-Grulich F.IIIs at Berlin-Staaken in 1923 and were taken over the following year by Deutscher Aero Lloyd, one of whose F.IIIs is seen landing past the Ahrens & Schulz flying school hangar at Hamburg-Fuhlsbüttel in 1924. Recorded as written off by Lufthansa with four other F.IIIs in July 1935, it was probably scrapped.

Deutsche Russische-Verkehrs GmbH (Deruluft) was established in 1921 and began services between Konigsberg and Moscow officially on 1 May 1922. Their first Fokker-built F.III, RR1, landed at Moscow-Chodynka on 30 April while RR3 arrived the following morning.

Lufthansa's Fokker-Grulich F.III D 575 *Isar* originally had a BMW IV engine, then changed to a BMW V, then back to a IV. From the very early days, before the founding of Lufthansa, aircraft carried the famous flying crane logo on the tail. This F.III seems to have been scrapped in July 1935.

An idyllic scene with Fokker-Grulich F.III D 594 *Fulda*, *c.*1930, at Reichenhall airfield with Udet Flamingo A 41 of the Fliegerschule Salzburg. The Flamingo subsequently returned to Germany as D-1041, while the F.III became D-OTIK in 1934 and was scrapped in 1935.

Loading cargo on Fokker-Grulich F.III D 468, an Armstrong Siddeley Puma-powered version. F.IIIs operated domestic freight services and some aircraft were still in use as late as 1936. D 468, however, was written off on 8 October 1926.

Dornier Komet III D 580 *Berlin-Köln* lands on a comparatively rough airfield. A slight puzzle here – it was originally Deutsche Aero Lloyd's *Berlin-Köln* and became Lufthansa's *Panther*, so this picture must have been taken before the name change. It was converted to a Dornier Merkur before passing to the German Flying School in 1934.

The Dornier Komet III was of similar layout to the Fokker F.III but with strutted wings. Aero Lloyd's D 552 *Frankfurt* was one of a number converted to Merkurs, becoming *Gepard* of Lufthansa, as seen in the picture below.

Here is D-552, having grown a hyphen, after conversion from the Komet III – above – to a Merkur and in Lufthansa colours as *Gepard*. Notable differences from the previous picture are the engine and propeller and, as a Merkur, it has a cut-out in the wing trailing edge. The route placard in the front window reads 'Berlin Essen/Mulheim'. The Rohrbach factory in the background suggests the location is Berlin-Staaken.

An historic photo showing passengers boarding a Lufthansa Komet III on 6 April 1926 for the inaugural service from Berlin to Zurich via Halle, Erfurt and Stuttgart. The aircraft is either D 580 or 585. If the latter, it was destroyed in a crash at Schleiz, Germany on 23 September 1927, killing the pilot and five passengers.

Deruluft's Dornier Merkur RR 30 at Königsberg, the starting point for the airline's service to Moscow. On 2 May 1927 the route was extended to Berlin. Note the 'Berlin-Moskau' notice in the cabin window. Deruluft had four Russian-registered Merkurs. In the background is D-1079 *Blaufuchs*, one of their German Merkurs which subsequently passed to Lufthansa. It crashed, location unknown, in November 1932.

Lufthansa was quick to realize the need for air cargo services and as early as 1928 operated a pure cargo network. Here, Dornier Merkur D 546 *Hyane* accepts freight from a Daimler-Benz van at Stuttgart-Boblingen Airport. Powered by a BMW VI engine, D 546 had been converted from a Komet III; it was retired in August 1933. The hyphen appears in the under wing registration but not on the fuselage.

A Junkers-F 13 is refuelled at Mannheim Airport with Fokker-Grulich F.III D 533 in the background. At this time the installation of tracks for the gasoline trolley was regarded as advanced. The Junkers is placarded to operate the 15.00 service to Karlsruhe.

An F 13 gets a thorough going over with its 185hp BMW IIIA engine, wings and tail surfaces removed. The thickness of the wing and its construction are apparent, as is the typical Junkers corrugated Duralumin skin.

It seems likely that F 13 D 1, Lufthansa's *Nachtigall*, was D 183 re-registered, since it shares the same constructor's number 531. Seen at Berlin at an unspecified date, D 1 was still is use there for pleasure flying at the outbreak of war in 1939.

No fancy starter on an F 13 – it had to be started by hand as demonstrated on D-203 *Bussard*. This aircraft participated in the 1923 Leipzig Spring Fair. Passed to the German Flying School at Berlin, it was re-registered D-ODEM.

Cleaners at work on an F 13. Note the carpet beater just above the Junkers badge. Access to the engine was made very easy, with the whole cowling moving upwards and backwards.

Breslau Airport in the grim winter of 1928-1929 showing the F 13 D-338 *Nebelkrähe* on skis. The conversion from a normal wheeled undercarriage could be carried out relatively quickly. In 1932 this aircraft went to the German Flying School in Berlin and was subsequently re-registered D-OVAS.

As a complete contrast to the previous scene, here is a pastoral setting for F 13 D-ONIL, formerly D-464 *Laubsänger*. Passengers watching the cameraman are in a heated cabin and their seats have safety belts, but the pilots have only a small windscreen.

Local colour as F 13 R-RECC of Junkers Luftverkehr Persien (LVP) poses at Teheran Airport c.1927; LVP ceased operations in 1932. The first F 13s to arrive at Teheran, in 1923, were military versions with a dorsal machine-gun position just behind the cockpit.

The Syndicato Condor was founded on 1 December 1927 in Rio de Janeiro, in Brazil, with Lufthansa participation, exclusively operating German-built aircraft. In a typical setting is F 13 P-BAJA *Iguassu*, the former D-347, one of four F 13s operated by Condor, initially on coastal services from Natal to Rio and Buenos Aires but the airline later expanded these into the interior.

Lufthansa provided equipment and staff for the German-Chinese airline Eurasia Aviation Corporation, founded on 19 September 1930. Initial equipment was F 13s, whose strength and reliability were great assets when flying over mountainous country with few landing grounds – most of the flat areas became a morass in the rainy season. Eurasia later spread across China with Junkers-W 33s and Ju 52/3Ms.

On 1 May 1931 Lufthansa inaugurated a freight service between Berlin and Istanbul with F 13 D-724 *Kolkrabe*, shown over inhospitable terrain with a Bulgarian military escort, a Potez XVII, wearing apparently civil marks B-BPEK. The F 13 crashed in mountains at Echterpfuhl on 2 November 1932.

The odd-looking Focke-Wulf A 16 first flew in June 1924 and D 659, powered by a 75hp Siemens & Halske engine, was used by a Berlin publisher for newspaper transport. Re-engined with a 100hp S & H, it became an A 16C and was one of five used by Lufthansa with whom it became *Borkum*. Four passengers could be carried in the cabin, while the pilot's open cockpit had a crash pylon. Lufthansa withdrew the type in 1928.

The prototype Focke-Wulf A 17 Möwe D 1149 was delivered in 1928 to Norddeutsche Luftverkehr and subsequently passed to Nordbayerische Verkehrsflug before being acquired by Lufthansa and named *Bremen*. It seems unusual that the loading of passengers was taking place while the 420hp Gnôme Rhone Jupiter engine was running.

Lufthansa operated a total of ten A 17s on domestic and international routes. This is A 17A *Emden* with a 480hp Siemens Jupiter VI engine, photographed in Switzerland. Eight passengers could be carried with a crew of two. Note the wheeled oxygen bottle near the undercarriage.

A well-known group of clowns, the Fratellinis, disembark from A 17A D 1416 *Osnabrück* in Paris. The route board just above the Lignes Aeriennes baggage cart indicates the Paris-Saarbrücken-Frankfurt-Berlin service. The *gendarme* seems more interested in the cameraman!

A Lufthansa A 17, probably D 1430 *Hannover*, loading mail at Hamburg-Fuhlsbüttel in 1934 from what appears to be a Dixi van, a version of the Austin 7 built under licence by BMW. Once again, loading is carried out with the engine running and the loader and his colleague with the cart appear to be in imminent danger from the fast-running prop.

The next model of the Focke-Wulf Möwe was the A 29 which had the same wing as the A 17 but a 750hp BMW engine. Four of the five built were operated by Lufthansa and D 1757 *Friesland* was the first. All had been withdrawn by the end of 1934.

Next in the sequence of Focke-Wulf airliners was the A 32 Bussard. Lufthansa used two of the five built, and D 1910, built in 1930, was the first. This and the second, D 1942, were acquired by Lufthansa in 1934, by which time they had become D-OBES and D-ODUL respectively and operated the Bremen-Hannover-Erfurt-Nuremburg services. A little smaller than the A 17, they had 310hp Junkers L 5 engines and could carry six passengers.

Last and biggest of the Focke-Wulf Möwe series was the A 38. Four were built for Lufthansa in 1931: D 2073 was the first and all were used on European routes. Unlike earlier models, the A 38s had a tail wheel instead of a skid, partially recessed. The original engine was an uncowled 400hp Siemens Jupiter and there were seats for ten passengers. The crew consisted of two pilots and a radio operator.

The one-off Arado V 1 D-1594 was built in 1928 and used by Lufthansa as an experimental mail carrier. It made a number of long-distance flights, Berlin-Marseilles-Seville in fifteen hours, Berlin-Istanbul, then Berlin-Tenerife-Las Palmas.

The Arado V 1 at La Laguna Airport, near Santa Cruz de Tenerife in 1929 where it attracted considerable attention. Powerplant was a 500hp BMW Hornet driving a three-bladed metal propeller. The Arado crashed at Neuruppin, Germany, on 19 December 1929 with two fatalities.

Two
Crossing the Atlantic

Lufthansa had always been interested in links with South America from the early days of its predecessors. In 1919, with German participation and pilots, the Colombian airline Sociedad Colombo Alemana de Transportes Aereos (SCADTA) was founded with a pair of Junkers-F 13 floatplanes. Then, in 1924, Deutscher Aero Lloyd established the Condor Syndikat in Berlin to study the viability of South American operations and bought two Dornier Wal flying-boats.

In January 1927 Lufthansa formed the Syndicato Condor in Rio as a Brazilian airline, and the next step was to link Europe to South America across the South Atlantic. The first journey was made by the airship *Graf Zeppelin* in a cooperation between Lufthansa, Condor and Hapag. Leaving Friedrichshafen on 18 May 1930, it landed at Recife on 22 May and arrived in Rio three days later. Mail was flown by Lufthansa to Seville and transferred to the airship for onward transmission to Recife, where Condor took it to Rio and Buenos Aires. Later, the mail went to Friedrichshafen for loading straight on to the airship.

In November 1931 the twelve-engined Dornier Do X flying-boat, sponsored by Lufthansa and Condor, set out on a flight to South America. After various problems *en route*, including repairs after fire damage to the wing and hull repairs to damage suffered on take off, it arrived and carried out demonstrations in both South and North America.

Lufthansa was still interested in flying mail across the South Atlantic and carried out trials with an eight-tonne Dornier Wal flying-boat catapulted from the modified steamer *Westfalen*. Following their success, a ten-tonne Wal was used and eventually two further ships were bought.

For the first scheduled service on 3 February 1934 a Heinkel He 70 flew from Berlin-Tempelhof to Stuttgart with thirty-eight kilograms of mail, then via Marseilles to Seville where a Ju 52/3m took over and flew to Bathurst, British Gambia, via a stopover at Las Palmas. The *Westfalen* left Bathurst with the Dornier Do 18 *Taifun* on its catapult and, thirty-six hours later, *Taifun* was launched, landing at Natal, where a Junkers-W 34 floatplane took the mail to Rio and met a connecting flight to Buenos Aires. In the first year of this service, Lufthansa operated forty-seven flights to and from South America.

The first practical experience of ship and aircraft joint operation was a series of flights in 1927-1928 using the steamer *Lutzow* of Noordeutscher Lloyd and Junkers-F 13 D 298, here seen being hoisted aboard. It was used for pleasure flights.

The Dornier Do X was designed for transatlantic operation and was built at Altenrhein, Switzerland, making its first flight in 1929, hence the obviously arranged registration D-1929. Initially powered by twelve 525hp Siemens Jupiter engines, cooling problems led to their replacement by 600hp Curtiss Conquerors, as seen here.

A high standard of comfort was provided for Do X passengers; this is a part of the prototype's main deck. Up to 100 could be carried, but, early in the test programme, 169 were flown for an hour – the greatest number to fly in one aircraft at that time.

The Do X prototype flew with Lufthansa for a short period before transfer to the German aviation research and test institute DVL. Exhibited in the Deutschen Luftfahrt Museum in Berlin, it was destroyed during an air raid. Two more were built for Italy.

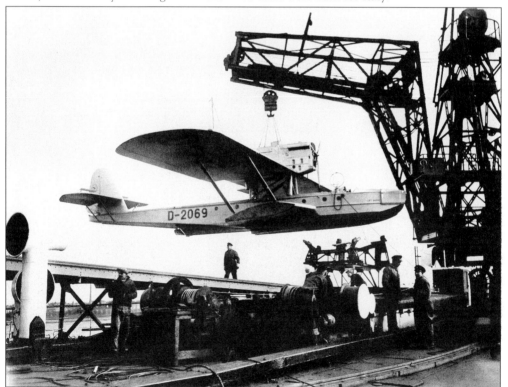

Trials were carried out in May 1929 at Bremerhaven with Dornier Do J 11 Wal D-2069, later named *Monsun*. Here it is being hoisted aboard the steamer *Westfalen* in the Elbe estuary for placing on the Heinkel-built K6 catapult.

The Wal sits on the *Westfalen*'s catapult during the Bremerhaven trials. When the flying-boat was used for passengers, fourteen could be carried in two cabins, but this example was a freighter.

On 6 June 1933, Wal D-2069 crossed the South Atlantic using the *Westfalen* as a stopover and catapult ship. On its return it was drawn back aboard by running onto a drag sail and was lifted back onto the catapult.

Wal D-2069 is catapulted from the
Westfalen in the first practical trials
at Bremerhaven. This was an eight-
tonne Wal with open cockpit and
two 600hp BMW engines. It was re-
registered D-ABIR in 1934.

A close-up of Wal D-2399 *Taifun*
on the *Westfalen*'s catapult showing
the operating gear. This was a
modified Wal with enclosed
cockpit, used on the first regular
airmail service between Germany
and South America on 3 February
1934.

When the airmail service began in 1934 a Heinkel He 70B flew mail to Seville or Larache, North Africa where it was transferred to a Junkers-Ju 52/3m which carried it to Bathurst, West Africa. There it was loaded on to a Dornier Wal for the Atlantic crossing. The aircraft here are He 70B D-UBAF *Sperber* and Ju 52/3m D-AKYS *Emile Thüy*. The latter eventually passed to Iberia as EC-AAH.

To shorten mail delivery across the North Atlantic, Lufthansa commissioned Heinkel to build a K2 catapult for installation on the Noorddeutscher Lloyd liner *Bremen*. A two-seat Heinkel He 12, D-1717, owned by the shipping company was operated by Lufthansa and is shown leaving the catapult off Cherbourg on its return from New York where it had been named after that city. It crashed on 6 October 1931.

Heinkel improved on the He 12 and built the He 58 D-1919 *Bremen* for use from the liner *Europa* which had been fitted with a K4 catapult. The later aircraft had a 450hp BMW Hornet engine, a licence-built version of the He 12's Pratt &Whitney Hornet. It made twenty-four flights in 1930 and was replaced in 1932 by the Junkers-Ju 46.

Junkers built two Ju 46 mail-carrying floatplanes for Lufthansa to replace the He 12 and He 58. Painted red and white, they were D-2244 *Europa* and D-2271 *Bremen* and were carried on the liners of those names. The Ju 46 was a modified and strengthened W 34 and had an uncowled 600hp BMW Hornet engine. D-2271 was eventually converted to a landplane and sold to Condor as PP-CAU.

Lufthansa eventually received a third Ju 46 floatplane, perhaps to replace the one sold to Condor. Painted red and white like the first two, it was originally allocated D-3411 but may not have worn these marks, becoming D-UBUS and also named *Europa*. Unlike the original *Europa* it had a cowled engine.

Dornier Do 18s were ordered to succeed Wals for ocean operations: the prototype was D-AHIS *Monsun* which flew on 15 March 1935. It had two 540hp Junkers Jumo engines, while production aircraft had 600hp Jumos. North Atlantic trials with Do 18s began in September 1936.

The first two Do 18s used by Lufthansa on the North Atlantic routes were D-ARUN *Zephir* and D-ABYM *Aeolus*; both were later transferred to the South Atlantic. Note the different engine installation to the prototype D-AHIS.

Dornier Do 18E D-AROZ *Pampero* of Lufthansa being recovered with hull well down to its parent ship. It was lost in a crash off Bathurst on 1 October 1938 with five fatalities. Lufthansa operated a total of six Do 18s of four different series.

The airship *Graf Zeppelin* first crossed the South Atlantic non-stop from Seville to Recife, Brazil, on 18 May 1930. On 20 March 1932 it entered regular service between Friedrichshafen and Recife every other week between April and October. It is seen here at Berlin-Staaken.

Lufthansa aircraft operated connecting mail flights with the *Graf Zeppelin* to cut shipment time. Airship flights continued until 1937 when the sister ship *Hindenburg* was destroyed by fire at Lakehurst, New Jersey. The *Graf Zeppelin* is seen here at its anchor mast in a tropical setting at Recife.

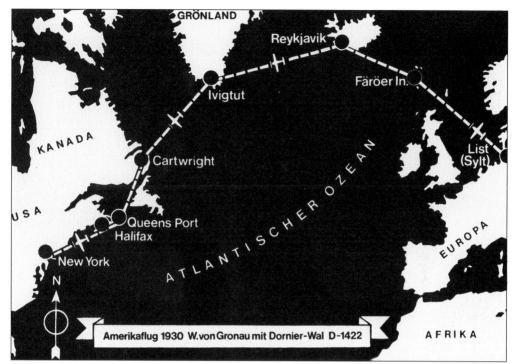

Lufthansa's interest in North Atlantic operations was stimulated by Wolfgang von Gronau's flight in Dornier Wal D-1422 from List to New York between 18 and 26 August 1930. Gronau was the director of the sea-flying schools at Warnemünde and List (Sylt), founded in 1925 by Junkers and Aero Lloyd.

Gronau's Wal D-1422 moored on the Hudson River, New York in front of the famous skyline after his North Atlantic crossing. The Wal was exhibited in 1932 in the Deutsches Museum, Munich, but was destroyed later in an air raid.

Following Do 18 trial flights across the North Atlantic, Lufthansa carried out fourteen services between August and November 1937 with the depot ships *Schwabenland* and *Friesenland* using two Blohm und Voss Ha 139 four-engined seaplanes, D-AMIE *Nordmeer* and D-AJEY *Nordwind*. The latter is seen here following redesign of its original circular fins and rudders.

Being prepared for launch, Ha 139 D-AMIN *Nordmeer* sits on the depot ship *Schwabenland*'s catapult. The Ha 139s had 605hp Junkers Jumo diesel engines which gave a cruising speed of 260km/h and maximum range of 5,300km.

For a third series of North Atlantic tests, the two Ha 139s were joined by a third, D-ASTA *Nordstern*. This had a 2.5m greater wing span with increased area and a slightly higher top speed. The three aircraft made twenty-six Atlantic crossings in 1938 but on the outbreak of war the following year all three were commandeered by the Luftwaffe for reconnaissance, mine laying and mine detection.

In 1937 Lufthansa ordered three Dornier Do 26 long-range flying-boats with which they hoped to operate a Lisbon-New York service. It was an exceptionally clean design, and the prototype, D-AGNT *Seeadler*, flew on 21 May 1938. It was powered by four 600hp Junkers Jumo engines and in place of sponsons used on earlier Dornier flying-boats, had retractable floats beneath the wings.

Preparations being made to lift Do 26 D-AGNT onto the depot ship *Friesenland*'s catapult. The mooring arrangements in the nose are clearly visible. Lufthansa's two Do 26s (the third, D-ASRA, was not completed when the war broke out) made eighteen crossings of the South Atlantic. The third Do 26, three new-build and Lufthansa's D-AWDS were militarized and used by the Luftwaffe in Norway where two were shot down on 28 May 1940 by Hurricanes.

Seeadler on the *Friesenland*'s K10 catapult, built by Heinkel at Rostock. The Do 26 normally carried a crew of five and the passenger cabin could take four. Had it entered service, the fares would probably have been extremely high with such a small load.

The functional and very clean, probably brand-new, cockpit of a Do 26. The pilot's clock (left hand controls) is mounted in the centre of the control wheel, while the co-pilot's is at the top of his instrument panel. The small door below the engine controls gave access to the mooring hatches and must have required a very small crewman!

Lufthansa's second Do 26, D-AWDS *Seefalke* was completed at the beginning of 1939 and had the more powerful 700hp Junkers Jumo engines. The rear ones could be raised, as in this view, to avoid spray when taking off and then lowered into position in flight.

Lufthansa's first four-engined landplane airliner was the Focke-Wulf Condor, first flown in July 1937. A pre-production aircraft, D-ADHR, showed its potential in a flight from Berlin to Salonica and Cairo. Lufthansa initially received six for domestic operations from summer 1938. In collaboration with Focke-Wulf, Condor D-ACON with extra tankage and a Lufthansa crew flew non-stop from Berlin-Staaken to Floyd Bennett Field, New York in twenty-four hours and fifty-seven minutes on 10-11 August 1938. Here it taxies in on its two outboard 720hp BMW engines.

Another view of Condor D-ACON (note the obviously fixed registration) emphasizing the clean lines of this all-metal airliner which could carry up to twenty-six passengers in two cabins. This aircraft was lost off Manila on 6 December 1938, allegedly due to fuel mismanagement.

54

The interior of a Condor, in this case OY-DEM *Jutlandia*, one of two supplied to Danish Air Lines. It managed to survive the war and, at some time, made its way to England, being dismantled at Northolt in 1947 following tailwheel damage. This is the rear cabin, while smokers were in the forward cabin, behind the cockpit. Note the step necessary to clear the main spar.

An evocative scene at Berlin-Tempelhof of Lufthansa's Condor D-AMHC *Nordmark*. The airline eventually operated twelve Condors and one special VIP version, D-2600, was used by Hitler. *Nordmark* was written off at an unrecorded location in 1943.

Condor D-AETA *Westfalen* comes in to land. The long-travel retractable tailwheel is noteworthy. This was the second prototype and was powered by 720hp BMW 132 engines. With modifications, the type was used by the Luftwaffe as a transport. With armament it also became a formidable anti-shipping aircraft in the Battle of the Atlantic.

Obviously impressed by the Condor, the Brazilian Syndicato Condor ordered two, PP-CBI *Abaitara* and PP-CBJ *Arumami* which were delivered in 1939 with 720hp Pratt &Whitney Hornet engines. *Abaitara*, shown at Rio's Santos Dumont Airport, was later purchased by Cruzeiro, and was damaged beyond repair by a DC-3 on 8 March 1947.

Three
Back to Europe

Slightly overlapping and ahead of its chronological order came the Focke-Wulf Condor. The reason for this was its Berlin-New York flight which effectively spelled the end of Lufthansa's transatlantic seaplane operations when a landplane showed what could be done in terms of long-range flights. It is impossible to say how this would have developed if the outbreak of war had not intervened, but the Condor's flight was a remarkable landmark in the development of Lufthansa and long-distance flying. These could then begin to be measured in hours against days by ocean liners.

We left the previous chapter after a run-down of transatlantic operations so now let's look at some of the early scenes in Germany. Little has been said so far about the development of airports, so we begin this chapter with a few pictures depicting operations at the Berlin airports.

After the end of the second building phase in 1928, Berlin-Tempelhof was the starting point for many Lufthansa domestic and European services. On the tarmac in front of the smart new terminal are Junkers-G 31 D-1722, Rohrbach Roland II D-1729 and Junkers-F 13 D-225.

Berlin-Tempelhof opened in 1923 and became Lufthansa's home base when the airline was formed in 1926. Looking more like a bus stop than an airport check-in area, this 1926 view shows the first temporary waiting rooms for Lufthansa passengers at Berlin.

Passenger service at the Lufthansa counter in 1926 in what appears to be a converted hangar. However, this temporary set-up would not last long.

Berlin-Tempelhof's main entrance at the end of 1928 with a smart limousine delivering passengers. But is the chap with his foot on the running-board carrying a coal scuttle?

Early Lufthansa courtesy buses carried no fewer than thirty-two destinations on their roof boards. Here they await passengers from either Fokker-Grulich F II D 784 or Junkers-G 24 D 879.

Berlin-Tempelhof's waiting and departure lounge, c.1928. Pleasure and special flights could be booked at the left-hand counter, departures went through doors at the right, while the flight board is to the right of departures.

A mixture of types on the Tempelhof tarmac. In the foreground is the Bristol Lucifer-engined Udet U 8 D 670, then Lufthansa Dornier Merkur D 596 *Wildkatze* and a Fokker-Grulich F.II, plus three Fokker F.IIIs of Deutsche Luft-Reederei with Danzig registrations, Dz 8, 5 and 10. In the distance, a line-up of Junkers-F 13s.

Lufthansa operated a vast maintenance base at Berlin-Staaken airport where aircraft were overhauled and repaired. Here, the BMW Hornet engines of Junkers-G 31 D-1786 *Westmark* are being serviced. Even in those early days, about 40,000 spares were stocked.

A complete overhaul of Rohrbach Roland I D-1327 *Hohentwiel* at Berlin-Staaken with the inner section of the wing being re-covered, hence the missing 7 of the registration. The Roland was re-registered D-APIN in 1934. In the left background is a dismantled Junkers-F 13.

Lufthansa received the prototype Rohrbach Roland D 991 in 1926, followed by five production aircraft in 1927. Early models had this open cockpit and metal propellers on the wing-mounted BMW engines.

The second Roland, D 999 *Watzmann*, with wooden propeller blades and open cockpit. Rolands began operating between Berlin and London via Hannover and Amsterdam in 1927 and the following year flew the Geneva, Zurich, Munich and Vienna routes.

Passengers aboard Roland D 999 were able to open the windows for farewells; the route board is beneath the open window. D 999 later went to Iberia as M-CBBB and was used on the Madrid-Barcelona service.

Roland I D-1280 *Feldberg* with metal propellers at Croydon in 1926. Ten passengers could be carried and, by 1931, Rolands were operating on seven Lufthansa routes. This one was sold to Iberia as M-CAEE.

Loading skis aboard a Roland which was being refuelled on a snowy tarmac. The skis seem to be going through the passenger door rather than the triangular freight door. The painting on the small door is an interesting detail.

The first Roland II was D-1692 *Stolzenfels* and featured an enclosed cockpit. Lufthansa had nine of this model, three of which – D-1712, D-1729 and D-1735 – subsequently went to Deruluft. The first of these was destroyed by fire in March 1935, while the other two were later re-registered D-ANUZ and D-AVOK respectively; *Stolzenfels* became D-ARAF. Rolands served Lufthansa until 1935.

Lufthansa ordered three Rohrbach Romar flying-boats for proposed transatlantic operations, and this is probably the first one, D-1693. It had three 500hp BMW engines driving pusher propellers, while the third, Romar II D-1747, had 750hp BMWs and could carry sixteen passengers. Proving unsuitable for transoceanic flights, they were used on Baltic services from 1929 but were out of service by 1933.

With four 450hp Napier Lion engines, the Dornier Super Wal D-1337 *Pottwal* was one of six operated by Lufthansa from 1928 on the Lübeck-Copenhagen-Göteborg-Oslo and Berlin-Stettin-Kalm-Stockholm routes. Engine spares must have been a problem since the six aircraft were fitted with four different types. Up to eleven passengers could be carried.

The Messerschmitt M 20 was developed from the smaller M 18 and first flew in February 1928. Lufthansa bought fourteen for its European routes, introducing them in 1929. This is the fifth aircraft, D-2005 *Odenwald* which, after re-registration as D-UNAH, crashed in Germany in 1936.

Lufthansa's tenth Messerschmitt M 20 was D-2290 *Fläming*. The type could accommodate ten passengers and had a crew of two. The 25.5 meters cantilever wing is noteworthy. Originally powered by a 500hp BMW engine, a number of M 20s were later re-engined with 640hp BMWs. Like D-2005, this one was also re-registered, becoming D-UXYN before crashing in Germany in 1937.

Junkers-Ju 46 seaplanes were mentioned earlier; Lufthansa also operated two landplane freighters in 1933. The second of these was D-2491 *Sirius* with a cowled 650hp BMW 132 engine. The type was in service until 1939.

Beginning in 1932, Ju 46 seaplanes operated Lufthansa coastal services in the north of Germany and the Baltic Sea. The type was readily converted from landplane to seaplane as may be seen by this study of D-2491 following conversion some time after 1934, when it was re-registered D-OBRA.

Another view of D-OBRA indicates the pleasant conditions under which coastal services could be operated from small jetties on a very personal basis. In the interval between being D-2491 and D-OBRA, it was D-UHYL for a time.

As early as 1928 Lufthansa recognized the potential of cargo by air and was soon operating an all-cargo network. Here is Junkers-W 33 D-1695 *Balkan* being loaded from a Lufthansa van. Passed to Eurasia in January 1933, this aircraft was destroyed at Shanghai in a Japanese bombing raid in August 1937.

Looking very new on a snow-covered airfield, Lufthansa Junkers-W 34 D-2394 *Castor* was one of at least eight used by the airline; it subsequently became D-OJOH. More than seventy W 34s were built with a variety of engines and the type was used on cargo services from the winter of 1932-1933.

The Junkers-G 23, flown in 1924, was the first three-engined all-metal monoplane to enter airline service and was the immediate forerunner of the heavier and more powerful G 24. This is the cabin of a G 24 which even had a neat toilet at the rear.

Although Lufthansa did not operate the Junkers-G 23, they bought some twenty-six G 24s from 1926 for international routes, and one was used in South America. A survey flight by two, D 901 *Tyr* and D 903 *Hera* was made from Berlin via Moscow and Irkutsk to Peking in August 1926 to study the possibility of a route to the Far East via Siberia. Here the G 24s are welcomed on their return to Berlin-Tempelhof on 26 September 1926.

An atmospheric study of Lufthansa's G 24 D 901; by this time it had been renamed *Ostmark*. There were more than twenty variants of the type, mostly with 280/310hp Junkers L 5 engines. This G 24 was destroyed in November 1933.

The simple cockpit of the G 24 was designed for two pilots with the main instruments on the central console. Cockpit comfort was minimal and with no soundproofing or lining the corrugated sides were easily visible.

On 1 May 1926 Lufthansa began the world's first night-flying passenger service between Berlin and Königsberg using a G 24. Here it is running up its outer engines prior to departure with the centre propeller still stationary. The strangely placed exhaust pipe for this engine can be seen extending over the cabin roof.

A Lufthansa shuttle bus meets G 24 D 1019 *Rotterdam* at Berlin-Tempelhof and takes them direct to the city centre. Although the aircraft had seats for nine passengers there are $10\frac{1}{2}$ here! This G 24 was originally H-NADB and S-AAAK before acquisition by Lufthansa.

In an unusual move, Junkers converted eleven G 24s to single-engine F 24s, deleting the wing centre section and reducing the span by four metres. Nine were converted from Lufthansa G 24s and returned to them. Comparison with the photograph above shows D-1019 (now with a hyphen) after conversion. It had a 520hp Junkers Jumo 4 diesel engine and still carried nine passengers. It was written off in April 1934.

Another G 24 converted to F 24 was D 1020 *Essen*, seen at Essen-Mulheim with a Junkers-G 38 on final approach. *Essen* began life with three Junkers L 2 engines, was later fitted with different BMW variants and ended up with a Jumo 4. In 1934 it was re-registered D-URIS.

Lufthansa's G 24 D 950 *Persephone* eventually passed to Syndicato Condor in Brazil, becoming P-BAHA *Potyguar* and was converted to seaplane configuration. Operating conditions here appear to be less than perfect!

Developed from the Junkers-G 24, the G 31 was larger and heavier. Lufthansa bought seven, the first being D 1310, seen here at Croydon; note the long exhaust pipe for the centre Gnome Rhône Jupiter engine. It was eventually re-registered D-ADIN.

Another view of G 31 D 1310 at Croydon on the floodlit tarmac. Here it is named *Hermann Köhl* but, at various times, was also *H Köhl* and *Deutschland*. Extending below the port wing tip are two flares for taxying at night. Lufthansa was the world's first airline to serve food and drink on board; standard passenger accommodation was fifteen, but D 1310 had eleven seats and increased range.

The first production Junkers-G 31 was D 1137, seen at Zurich-Dubendorf Airport. Although it did not enter service with Lufthansa (their first G 31 was the second production aircraft D 1310) the photo is of interest as it shows the open cockpit fitted to some aircraft.

Lufthansa was keen to develop de-icing equipment in order to operate in extreme weather conditions, but in the early days a man with a broom, as shown clearing snow from G 31 D-1523 *Nordmark* at Croydon, was the only answer.

When, in May 1928, Lufthansa introduced the G 31 it became the first airline to serve food and drinks in flight. The cabin was reminiscent of a railway carriage with its string luggage racks but it was a welcome innovation to be fed *en route*.

A one-off design from the Udet-Flugzeugbau at Munich-Rangsdorf was the U 11 Kondor D 828. Four 100hp Siemens & Halske Sh 12 engines drove pusher propellers and there were eight seats in the passenger cabin; the crew of three had to make do in an open cockpit. The Kondor was with Lufthansa from 1926 to 1928, but in what capacity is not known. It was scrapped in 1931.

The massive Junkers-G 38 D-2000 flew at Dessau on 6 November 1929 and, following a number of modifications, was delivered to Lufthansa in June 1930. The second aircraft, D-2500, followed in September 1931 and is seen flying over the Dornier Do X D-1929 moored on the Ausseralster, Hamburg – an interesting view of the two largest aircraft at that time.

As noted above, the G 38 was the world's largest landplane in 1929 with a wing span of more than 144ft and length of 76ft. Clearly shown are the double undercarriage wheels and full-span flaps. In 1932 D-2500 was re-engined with four 800hp Junkers L 88as.

On 23 April 1933 the second G 38 was named *Generalfeldmarschall von Hindenburg* at Berlin-Tempelhof. This required the Lufthansa title to be moved back under the wing leading edge. The passenger cabins in the wing leading edges gave a splendid view forward but nothing sideways and must have been very noisy. Here is D-2500 at Halle/Leipzig Airport, probably on a demonstration.

For such a large aircraft the G 38 had a remarkably spartan and primitive cockpit. As in earlier Junkers transports, there was no lining to hide the corrugated construction. Note the large number of knobs protruding from the central console!

The first G 38 D-2000 after re-registration as D-AZUR and now wearing the name *Deutschland*. There are no spinners on the propellers and a piece of test equipment is apparent on the wing. At this time the swastika was on one side of the rudders with red and white bars on the other. This G 38 crashed on take off at Dessau in 1936.

The G 38 had a speed of 180km/h and a range of 2,000km. Passenger capacity in the four cabins and wing leading edges was thirty-four. Even the seating was spartan compared with other contemporary aircraft, but seat belts were provided. This is the view looking forward.

Re-registered D-APIS in 1934, D-2500 shares a tarmac, possibly at Berlin-Tempelhof, with Lufthansa Ju 52/3ms and a Ju 86 while Heinkel He 111 D-AXAV flies over. In that year, 750hp Junkers Jumo diesels were installed in place of the L 88as. Note the large tailwheel extending behind the fuselage.

Seen during one of its several visits to Croydon Airport, G 38 D-APIS then had swastikas on both sides of the rudders. Only this aircraft entered scheduled service with Lufthansa and it attended the opening of Stockholm-Bromma Airport on 23 May 1936. It was destroyed at Athens by RAF bombing while serving with the Luftwaffe as a troop transport marked GF+GG during the Second World War.

Developed from the single-engined Junkers-Ju 52, the tri-motor Ju 52/3m became the backbone of Lufthansa's fleet from 1933, the first two, D-2201 *Boelcke* and D-2202 *Richthofen* being delivered in May and September 1932. The type was introduced in summer 1933 between Berlin and London via Hannover and Amsterdam, and Berlin-Rome via Munich and Venice. Lufthansa's third Ju 52/3m and the seventh production aircraft was D-2468, re-registered D-AFIR in 1934.

Taxying at Berlin-Tempelhof is Ju 52/3m D-3049 *Heinrich Gontermann*, probably in 1933 as it became D-ALAS the following year. Lufthansa operated more than 230 examples of the type between 1939 and 1945, many with the spatted undercarriage as shown here. Seating seventeen passengers, the Ju 52/3m could cruise at 250km/h and had a range of 900km.

Paris-Le Bourget Airport in May 1939 with air raid shelters being dug alongside the passenger terminal. On the tarmac are Imperial Airways' D.H. Albatross G-AFDK, KLM's DC-2 PH-AKP and Lufthansa's Ju 52/3m D-ARAM *Werner Voss*, formerly D-3131. It was to be another sixteen years before British, Dutch and German airliners were to meet.

Lufthansa's involvement with the Syndicato Condor in Brazil led to that airline operating twenty-one Ju 52/3ms including some floatplane versions such as PP-CBB *Tupan*. Maintenance is being carried out here in a floating dock in Buenos Aires harbour.

Ju 52/3m D-ASIS *Wilhelm Cuno* at Croydon in the mid-1930s. While early versions had 525-600hp BMW Hornet engines, later models were fitted with a variety of makes, including the Bristol Pegasus and Pratt & Whitney Hornet and Wasp; most powerful was the 830hp BMW 132T.

Basically a landplane version of the Ha 139 (see pages 50-51), the Ha 142 was intended for transatlantic mail flights and four were built for Lufthansa. The prototype, D-AHFB – a fixed registration denoting the manufacturer's former name Hamburger Flugzeugbau – flew on 11 October 1938. It was later given a second fixed registration, D-ABUV, indicating the new company name of Blohm und Voss, and then became the Bv 142.

The Bv 142 D-ABUV *Kastor* in Lufthansa colours. It made a few exploratory flights but nothing came of the transatlantic proposals and it was returned to Blohm und Voss. Following conversion for military reconnaissance work it and three other prototypes were handed over to the Luftwaffe.

An engine run for Bv 142 D-ABUV on a bright summer day. It had four BMW 132H engines and each of them gave 880hp. All undercarriage units had twin wheels. Note the strange siting of the braced tailplane on a pillar above the rear fuselage.

Junkers' break with corrugated skin construction came in 1932 with the Ju 60 which the designer said had been 'rather too quickly developed.' After seventy-five test flights, totalling thirty-seven hours flying time, it was handed over to Lufthansa as D-2400 *Pfeil*, later D-UPAL. It had been ordered by the RVM, the German Transport Ministry, and not by the airline.

The interior of the Ju 60 showing the six passenger seats which would have required difficult manoeuvring for the unfortunate occupants. This view looks towards the tail from just behind the cockpit.

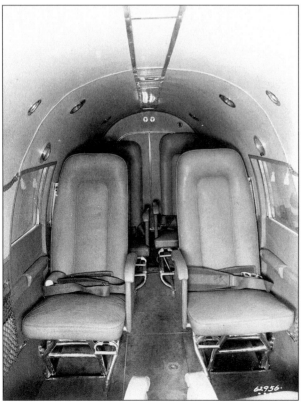

The Ju 60 had a 600hp BMW Hornet engine, a six-seat cabin and a crew of two in tandem; the undercarriage was partially retractable. It is thought to have been used by Lufthansa between Berlin and Athens on cargo flights in 1933, while it was in passenger service in 1934 from Berlin to Breslau, with other services the following year. Its fate is not recorded.

Directly developed from the Ju 60, the Ju 160 had a 660hp BMW 132E engine and a more roomy interior. This picture was taken from between the two front seats which faced rearwards.

Engine maintenance on a Ju 160, possibly D-UJYM *Nerz* judging from the top of the name just visible above the wing leading edge. In the background is Heinkel He 70 D-UMIM *Albatros*. The engine cowling hinged upwards to give easy access. The Ju 160 cruised at 310km/h.

Lufthansa Ju 160 D-UMEX *Panther* receives fuel and some last minute screw tightening. There seems to have been variations in the positioning of wireless aerials on the type, some of which were ahead of the cockpit, and *Panther* does not seem to have one.

As a contrast to the previous picture, Ju 160 D-UVOX *Rotfuchs* has an aerial ahead of the cockpit. The inwards retracting undercarriage was much neater than that on the Ju 60, and a tailwheel replaced the latter's skid. In the background is more of the Lufthansa fleet: Heinkel He 70 D-UJUZ *Bussard*, Junkers-F 24 D-UDOP *Bayern* and a Ju 52/3m.

Ju 160s D-UVOX *Rotfuchs* and D-UMEX *Panther* share the tarmac at Berlin-Tempelhof with Junkers-F 24 D-UMUR *Österreich*, originally built as a three-engined G 24, D 1016 for Lufthansa and converted along with eight others to F 24s in 1928. Landing in the background is Ala Littoria's Ju 52/3m I-BEZI.

The swept-back wing leading edge of the Ju 160 is well shown here on D-UGAZ *Iltis* awaiting crew and passengers with door and cockpit open. Behind is another of Lufthansa's nine F 24s, D-URIS, the former G 24 D 1020.

Ju 160 D-ULIK *Gepard* shares the Berlin-Tempelhof tarmac with Ju 86 D-AREV *Brocken* and Ju 52/3m D-AFYS *Gustav Doerr* and another, while a Junkers-G 24 is in the distant hangar. Lufthansa operated twenty-one Ju 160s from 1935, sixteen of which were still in service when war began in 1939.

Lufthansa commissioned Heinkel in 1932 to produce a high-speed four-passenger aircraft after seeing the Lockheed Orion ordered by Swissair. Heinkel's offering was the He 70, which flew on 1 December 1932. Lufthansa received the second aircraft and this is the third, D-3114 *Sperber*, later D-UBAF.

The He 70 was beautifully streamlined, had a fully-retractable undercarriage and was powered by a 630hp BMW VI engine. The neat cowling and uncomplicated undercarriage with wheel covers are well shown in this view of D-UDAS *Habicht* on the tarmac at Croydon.

The He 70's four-seat cabin was arranged with pairs facing, and doors for crew and passengers were in the starboard fuselage side. This is D-UDAS *Habicht* again. In the spring of 1933 the second He 70 set eight speed records and reached almost 222mph, being claimed as the fastest passenger aircraft in Europe.

The cockpit of an He 70 was offset to port on the prototype and the He 70A and B, but on the centreline for other models. The radio operator was slightly below and to the right of the pilot.

Clean lines of the He 70 are apparent on Lufthansa's D-UMIM *Albatros*. The airline began passenger services on so-called Blitz routes with D-UDAS *Habicht* on 15 June 1934 linking Berlin with Hamburg, Cologne and Frankfurt, operating a total of fourteen. All were withdrawn from service in 1938.

An evocative scene shows He 70 D-UPYF *Adler* in front of the Essen-Mulheim terminal and restaurant as a Ju 52/3m flies over. Three of the He 70s were lost, D-AHUX crashed on 3 November 1934 near Carcassonne, France, D-UXUV crashed on take-off at Stuttgart on 20 May 1937 with four fatalities, and an unidentified one crashed near Wiesbaden on 25 April 1935, killing one occupant.

Developed as an airliner and bomber, the Junkers Ju 86 was designed for diesel engines. Lufthansa operated sixteen, most with 600hp Jumo 205C diesels, although several were later re-engined. The fourth aircraft was D-AREV *Brocken*, seen on a busy Berlin-Tempelhof tarmac, *c.*1936, together with six Ju 52/3ms, two F 24s, a W 33, W 34, F 13, Ju 160 and He 70. Apparently swastikas on all the tails have been touched out!

The interior of a Ju 86 was reasonably comfortable, accommodating ten passengers and a crew of two. Seats were slightly staggered and turned inwards to give more space since the cabin width was only 1.45m (4ft 9in).

Two Lufthansa Ju 86s, D-AQER *Inselberg* and D-AKOI *Kaiserstuhl*, in front of the Lufthansa maintenance base at Hamburg. There has been some retouching to remove the swastika tail markings.

Moving to the right of the previous photograph we can see the same Ju 86 receiving attention to its starboard engine while in the background – complete with its swastika – is Ju 160 D-UBIQ *Silberfuchs*. Some Ju 86s were used for cargo flights, but only one remained by 1940.

Following the success of the Heinkel He 70, Lufthansa decided to order a larger aircraft and the He 111 was born. Its lines were very reminiscent of its predecessor and it attracted the attention of the German Air Ministry who ordered bomber versions. The transport prototype flew in early 1935 as D-ALIX *Rostock* and was delivered to Lufthansa. It is seen here at Berlin-Tempelhof with another, D-AXAV, flying over. The censor has again deleted all swastika tail markings. Used on some sectors of the South Atlantic mail service, D-ALIX crashed in a swamp near Bathurst, Gambia, on 12 March 1937 with four fatalities.

He 111D-ABYE *Königsberg*, again at Berlin-Tempelhof, was an early delivery to Lufthansa. Powered by two 750hp BMW VI engines, it cruised at almost 190mph and was introduced on some of the airline's domestic express routes in 1936.

While the prototype He 111 had the fully glazed nose of the bomber version, the airliners had a stepped nose with separate cockpit, with a mail compartment in place of the bomb aimer's position. A vintage BMW van brings the baggage for loading on a snow-covered tarmac.

Although Lufthansa's He 111s could carry ten passengers in two cabins at a high cruising speed, the type was not economic and the airline only used twelve intermittently until September 1939. Before the outbreak of war, D-ALIX and D-AHAO equipped with cameras were used, ostensibly on route-proving flights, over Britain, France and Russia, but were actually on reconnaissance duties.

Appearing to be a four-engine version of the He 111, the He 116 was in fact slightly smaller. A long-distance mail-plane with a range of almost 2,800 miles, it was intended for Lufthansa's South Atlantic and Middle East routes and D-AJIE *Schlesien* was the prototype which did not enter regular service. Lufthansa had two others, D-ATIO *Hamburg* and D-ARFD *Rostok*, all with 240hp Hirth HM508 engines. *Hamburg* crashed near Langeoog on 27 May 1938 with three fatalities.

As a development of the Ju 89 bomber, Junkers built the Ju 90 airliner, with four 1,100hp Daimler-Benz DB 600 engines, and flew the prototype, D-AALU, on 7 June 1937. The second, D-AIVI *Preussen*, had 830hp BMW 132H engines which became standard on production aircraft. It crashed on take-off at Bathurst, Gambia, during tropical trials on 26 November 1938 with sixteen fatalities.

A night scene as Ju 90 D-AIVI *Preussen* prepares for take-off; note the landing light in the nose. The presence of a military Ju 86 in the background suggests that the location may be the manufacturer's airfield at Dessau.

The third Ju 90 was D-AURE *Bayern* which entered service on the Berlin-Vienna route in 1938. It is seen running up with the cabin door and cockpit windows open. It was destroyed in an air raid on Stuttgart, probably on 5 September 1944 when USAAF B-17s attacked targets said to include an aero-engine plant.

Bayern makes a low fly-past, presumably being demonstrated to the press. The sleek lines of the Ju 90 and the full span flaps are visible. Once again the censor has obliterated the swastika marking on the fin; this would have been a post-war edict.

The Ju 90 passenger cabin had luxurious seating for up to forty with windows in pairs and there were two toilets, cloakrooms and mail and baggage compartments depending on the layout used. Light luggage racks of steel tubing were above the seats and steward/stewardess service was provided.

The BMW engines of the Ju 90 could be changed quite easily, with the propellers still in place. The mobile loading ramp is interesting, as is the rather strange-shaped door behind the cockpit. In the background is the Siemens factory.

The cockpit of the Ju 90 was neat and functional – a Junkers trademark was the corrugated panel behind the pilot's seat! Visibility was good, and the crew was four or five – a second seat can be seen behind the co-pilot. Lufthansa operated eleven Ju 90s, several of which were handed over to the Luftwaffe on the outbreak of war.

A requirement for a fast, retractable undercarriage airliner to compete on European routes led Lufthansa to buy two Boeing 247s in 1934: D-AGAR and D-AKIN (tested in US marks as NC90Y and NC91Y). They had ten-seat passenger cabins and a crew of three. Engines were 550hp Pratt & Whitney Wasps.

Baggage and cargo compartments were divided in the Boeing 247; that in the rear cabin had a 65cu.ft capacity while the nose compartment offered 60cu.ft. The main cabin was 20ft long and 6ft high with a toilet and pantry at the rear.

A Lufthansa Boeing 247, probably at Amsterdam-Schiphol. Cruising at 155mph, the type was an immediate success in the USA, but Lufthansa was the only European operator and an expected order for a third did not materialize. Both were lost in accidents, D-AGAR at Nuremburg on 24 May 1935 when it was struck by a taxiing Air France aircraft, and D-AKIN in a crash at Hannover on 13 August 1937.

A Boeing 247 cockpit. Flight instruments used by both pilots are in the centre, while engine and fuel system indicators are in front of the co-pilot in the right seat. Lufthansa's initial contact with Boeing could not have foreseen the airline's big orders for Boeing aircraft delivered over the last forty years of the twentieth century.

A number of Czech Airlines' Douglas DC-3s were seized during the war and operated by Lufthansa. This Fokker-assembled example, D-AAIG, was formerly OK-AIG and wears Lufthansa titles on the nose. It crashed off Frederikstad, Norway, on 21 April 1944, by a strange coincidence the same day that BOAC DC-3 G-AGFZ crashed on landing at Bromma, Sweden.

The interior of a 1940s DC-3. While not necessarily the same layout as a Czech aircraft, it gives a good idea of the standard of comfort afforded passengers at the time, with curtained windows and attractive ceiling fittings and baggage racks.

KLM's Douglas DC-2 PH-AKT *Tockan* was captured by the Luftwaffe in May 1940 and became NA+LA, the personal aircraft of General Christeansen, Wehrmacht commander in the Netherlands. It was later passed to Lufthansa, becoming D-AIAV, but was written off at Lammershagen on 9 August 1940.

Lufthansa acquired a number of Fokker-assembled DC-2s before the war. This is D-ABEQ *Taunus*, formerly PH-AKF, delivered in 1935. Sold to LOT Polish Airlines as SP-ASJ, it was destroyed in a crash in the Rhodope Mountains, Bulgaria, on 25 November 1937.

Four
Pilot Training

Little appears to have been published on the training of Lufthansa pilots between the wars, but it seems that most would have attended the many civilian flying schools that existed under the Deutsche Luftfahrt-Verband (German Aviation Association) founded in 1902. However, on 25 March 1933 the new German government formed a successor, the Deutscher Luftsportverband – DLV – (German Sports Flying Association). At this time the clandestine Luftwaffe was just coming into the open, so civilian and military pilots would probably have received basic training side-by-side in the flying schools using a variety of types. Famous fighter pilot Adolf Galland in his book *The First & the Last* (Methuen, 1954) recalls his first glider flights, then light aircraft and, after passing his last examination in Brunswick in 1933, being attached to Lufthansa as a voluntary pilot flying a Junkers-G 24 or Rohrbach Roland twice a week.

Lufthansa established a commercial flying school at Berlin-Staaken, and it was later suggested that the real purpose of the airline's night routes was to train Luftwaffe crews in night and blind flying since some of the airliners, such as the Ju 86 and He 111, were thinly disguised bombers.

An example of this training mentioned in *Luftwaffen Story 1935-1939* by Karl Ries (Verlag Dieter Hoffman, 1974) was the creation in November 1933 of the Reichsbahnstrecken (State Railway Routes), a cover name, which was to provide training in long-distance and blind-flying and navigation. An agreement with Lufthansa resulted in the creation in 1934 of the Verkehrsinspektion der Deutschen Lufthansa AG at Berlin and Tutow, with headquarters at Tempelhof. A total of five *Staffeln* was formed, and civil-registered aircraft used included a Ju W 33 and five Ju 52/3ms.

Post-war training was a different matter. In September 1953 a flight training school was opened in Cologne with ten ground instructors. Refresher flying training was provided in England by Air Service Training at Hamble, near Southampton. Pilots then went to the USA for manufacturers' training facilities for conversion on to Convair 340s and Super Constellations. In the winter of 1954-1955, Lufthansa began its own *ab initio* training at Hamburg using Saab Safirs. The trainees were pilots who already had thousands of hours military flying in their log books and the instructors were British. It was not until 5 May 1955 that the Federal Republic's sovereignty over its own airspace was restored and, in May 1956, the commercial pilots' school was moved to Bremen where it remains. Starting with the DHC Chipmunk, new types were introduced.

Lufthansa pilots trained in the 1930s at civilian flying schools would have flown a variety of types, typical of which was the Bücker Jungmann, first flown in April 1934, initially with an 80hp Hirth HM 60R engine, but later fitted with a 105hp Hirth HM 504. It entered large-scale production and was also licence-built in other countries. There are still many flying today.

Another important trainer of the 1930s on which many Lufthansa pilots would have cut their teeth was the Focke-Wulf Stieglitz with a 150hp Siemens Sh 14A engine. Built in large numbers in Germany and overseas, a few survive and the Lufthansa Historic Foundation is restoring one to flying condition. Bought from South Africa as ZS-WRI, it will become D-EQAX.

First flown in 1935, the Focke-Wulf Weihe was built as a six-seat light transport and crew trainer, powered by two 240hp Argus As 10C engines. Lufthansa used several: this one, D-OVXF *Elbe* had Hirth HM 508D engines.

106

This Lufthansa Focke-Wulf Weihe is in a smarter colour scheme and, to judge by the passengers, would probably have been used on an airline service. There is a handy step up to the wing root, the door seems remarkably thick and the wing strut is very obvious.

Post-war Lufthansa pilot training in Germany began on 1 May 1956 when the airline opened its flying school at Bremen. First equipment was the Saab Safir, two of which were bought. Here, at Hamburg, D-EBAB is checked over with the other Safir alongside, while in the background is Convair 340 D-ACAD.

The Bremen flying school soon added a fleet of nine DHC Chipmunks to its Safirs, a third of the latter having been bought. Students are here being briefed for a training flight with four Chipmunks lined up between two Safirs.

By June 1963, the Lufthansa Safirs had acquired full company colours, but were being replaced by Beech Debonairs. This particular Safir was built in the Netherlands by De Schelde at Dordrecht under sub-contract to Saab who had capacity problems at that time. The Dutch company produced 120; D-EBUC was subsequently sold as PH-RJB.

In mid-December 1956 two new Beech Twin Bonanzas were bought for instrument-flying instruction at the Bremen school and ferried from Wichita, Kansas, to Germany. The first, D-IDUK, flown by head of the flight training department Captain Walter Blume with Captain Schams took just over thirty-two hours and diverted to Hannover because of fog, while the second, D-IGIL, with Captains Utter and Sult took forty hours and thirty minutes in very bad weather.

The Twin Bonanzas were eventually replaced by Beech King Airs, D-ILHA being the first, in 1981. Lufthansa Boeing 737, 727 and Beech Debonair are in the background at Bremen. This King Air was retired in 1999 having run out of hours and was last seen at Hamburg devoid of registration.

Europe's unsettled weather conditions and heavy air traffic movements resulted in Lufthansa contracting with Pacific Southwest Airlines in 1967 for major flying training to be completed in the USA, with PSA providing technical facilities, aircraft and instructors. Initially at San Diego, the school moved to Phoenix, Arizona, in January 1970, using Beech Bonanzas and Barons.

The Bremen training school later re-equipped with Piper Senecas and Cheyennes for twin-engine work. Visiting Innsbruck during an open day at the airport is Cheyenne III D-IOSB, parked next to the SF.260s of the Italian Alpi Eagles aerobatic team.

Five

Post-war Services

It was to be ten years after the end of the war in Europe before German sovereignty over its own airspace was restored and the country could again begin to operate commercial services, initially with Douglas DC-3s.

At that time, the American industry was in the best position to supply airliners; there were plenty of surplus DC-3s and DC-4s available but in fact – apart from the DC-3s and several hired Vickers Vikings – Lufthansa chose new aircraft: Convair 340s and Lockheed Super Constellations, for its international routes.

By 1960 jet equipment was in service, with Boeing 707s opening routes to the Far East. These aircraft were to be the first of many orders which Lufthansa was to place with the American manufacturer for 727s, 737s and 747s. McDonnell Douglas DC-10s were also bought, while subsidiary Condor, in addition to the foregoing types – except 747s – bought Boeing 757s and 767s and Airbus A320s.

Celebrating its 50th anniversary in 1976, Lufthansa received its first Airbus A300 and its fleet has subsequently been increased to include all Airbus models except the A330. Lufthansa Cityline, formerly DLT, operates Avro and Canadair RJs, while Lufthansa Cargo Services, formerly German Cargo Services, has used DC-8s and 707s before re-equipping with McDonnell Douglas (now Boeing) MD-11s.

On 29 November 1954, Lufthansa's first post-war airliners, Convair 340s, arrived at Hamburg and on 1 April 1955 the airline began regular services with its new equipment. By mid-May it was back on its traditional routes to Paris and London, and on 16 May Convair D-ACOH began a regular service to London-Heathrow. Here it is with BEA DC-3s and an Ambassador in the background.

Lufthansa pilots had carried out instrument flying training on foreign-registered DC-3s in the winter of 1954-1955, but by October 1955 Lufthansa had three DC-3s of its own and introduced the type on domestic routes, keeping them until 1960. This is D-CADE, operated in a twenty-four-passenger layout.

Short of cargo capacity, Lufthansa leased Curtiss C-46 N9891Z in the mid-1960s and it became a familiar sight around Europe along with several operated by Norwegian carrier Fred Olsen.

Lufthansa soon resumed its North Atlantic services, and the first of four Lockheed Super Constellations arrived at Hamburg in mid-April 1955 on its delivery flight non-stop from New York in thirteen hours and forty-seven minutes. The first westbound service was flown on 15 August 1956 via Dusseldorf and Shannon. This is L.1049G D-ALAP.

Lufthansa's maintenance hangar, completed at Hamburg in 1954, could hold ten twin-engine or six four-engine aircraft. Here, in 1956, are four Super Constellations, D-ALAP, 'LEC, 'LEM and 'LOF, with a Convair at the far end.

Depending on layout, the Super Constellation could carry up to eighty-six passengers in a Lufthansa configuration. Engines were turbo-compound 3,250hp Wright R-3350s giving a 355mph cruising speed. The type served with Lufthansa until 1967. Here D-ALEC is framed by a Vickers Viscount.

The final Constellation development was the L-1649A Starliner which had a new wing of 27ft greater span and 3,400hp Wright 988TC engines. Known in Lufthansa service as the Super Star, it had the same passenger capacity as the L-1049G which it succeeded. This is D-ALOL, Lufthansa's fourth and last.

In October 1959 the first of nine Vickers Viscount 814s, D-ANUN, arrived at Hamburg for Lufthansa's European routes, and the Rolls-Royce Dart turboprop airliner initially supplemented and later replaced the Convairs. Lufthansa eventually operated eleven Viscounts but they began to be replaced by Boeing 737s in 1968 and five, including this one, were sold to Nora Air Services at Kassel.

Lufthansa entered the pure jet age with the arrival at a wet Hamburg of its first Boeing 707-430, D-ABOB, on 2 March 1960. The first service from there to New York was via Frankfurt and Gander. It was the first Boeing bought by the airline since the 247s in 1934 and was the beginning of a long relationship with the American manufacturer.

In early 1964 the first Boeing 727 arrived at Hamburg and in mid-April the type entered service on European and Near East routes. Christened Europa Jets, they were named after German towns and here D-ABIN *Münster* awaits passengers framed by the tail of D-ABIW *Bielefeld*. Both are Model 100s with 14,000lb thrust Pratt & Whitney JT8D engines giving a 575mph cruise with up to 107 passengers. Lufthansa later received Model 200s with 16,000lb thrust JT8Ds and seating up to 189 in tourist layout.

The next Boeing type for Lufthansa was the 737, and the first of an initial order for twenty-one arrived at Hamburg on 4 February 1968. These were known as City Jets, and D-ABHU *Konstanz* is seen at Frankfurt. The airline has operated several versions, the latest of which is the Series 500. Maximum capacity depending on variant is 109 passengers. This is a Series 200.

Lufthansa was the first European operator of the Boeing 747, costing about $80 million each, and took delivery of its first, D-ABYA, on 30 March 1970 at Hamburg. The airline was also the world's first to use the cargo 747F which entered service on the North Atlantic on 19 April 1972. As an example of its capacity, publicity photos show it with seventy-two Volkswagen Beetles. Lufthansa's 747Fs were powered by 52,500lb thrust General Electric CF-6 engines and the first was delivered to the airline on 10 March 1972.

The McDonnell Douglas DC-10 was Lufthansa's second wide-body jet and the first of nine arrived at Hamburg on 22 October 1973. At the beginning of 1974 the type entered service on the Frankfurt-Rio route and, by the summer, the four DC-10s delivered were serving South East Asia and Australia. Here, D-ADAO *Dusseldorf* is shown at Long Beach prior to delivery. For some reason, all Lufthansa DC-10 registrations ended in O.

The third wide-body type was the Airbus A300, the first being handed over on 9 February 1976 at the MBB factory at Hamburg-Finkenwerder as the commercial airport at Fuhlsbuttel was fogbound. It was a fitting marking of the airline's 50th anniversary. The 249-seat A300B-2 entered service on 1 April 1976 to Algiers and Dubai. This is the second to be delivered, D-AIAB *Rüdesheim am Rhein*. Powerplant was the General Electric CF6-50C.

Selecting the Airbus A310 to augment and gradually replace its Boeing 727s, Lufthansa ordered twenty-five on 2 April 1979 and took options on a further twenty-five. On 10 April 1983 the first entered service from Frankfurt to Stuttgart and by the beginning of 1984 eight had been delivered. The third, D-AICC, is seen, rather obviously, at Hamburg.

In the smaller single-aisle family, Lufthansa received its first Airbus A320 in October 1989, followed by the stretched A321-100 in January 1994 and the baby, the 124-seat A319-100, in July 1996. This was their first A319, D-AILA *Frankfurt (Oder)*. By late 1998, Lufthansa had seventy-three of this family in service replacing Boeing 737s.

The largest Airbus ordered was the A340, and by late 1998 Lufthansa had received six A340-200s and 12 '300s. This is Series 200 D-AIBA *Nürnberg* climbing out of the Airbus factory airfield at Toulouse-Blagnac on a pre-delivery flight wearing its test registration F-WWBE.

On 10 March 1977, Lufthansa established a subsidiary, German Cargo Services, for airfreight charter work. By mid-May the company had two ex-Lufthansa Boeing 707s while a third and fourth were added later. All were painted what was described as 'curry yellow'. Here is the first, D-ABUA, at Hong Kong-Kai Tak in 1977. In the background, a Kuwait Air Force DC-9, RAF Hercules and a pair of Cathay TriStars.

German Cargo replaced its Boeing 707s from 1985 with four McDonnell Douglas DC-8-73s refitted with fanjet engines by American company Cammacorp. Here are three, D-ADUI, 'DUE and 'DUO at the Frankfurt cargo base, showing some of the loading equipment needed for these operations. The DC-8s were replaced from 1998 by Boeing MD-11Fs.

The latest type to enter service with Lufthansa Cargo – as the company is now named – is the Boeing (formerly McDonnell Douglas) MD-11F freighter. Five have been bought, D-ALCA to 'LCE and they entered service in 1998: this is the second, D-ALCB. With General Electric CF6-80 engines, the MD-11F has a maximum payload of seventy-nine tons compared with the DC-8's forty-nine tons.

Founded on 31 October 1955 as Deutsche Flugdienst by Norddeutscher Lloyd, Hamburg-America Line, German National Railways and Lufthansa, the company became Condor Flugdienst in 1961 operating charters. Initially using Vickers Vikings, it received four Viscounts from Lufthansa in the 1960s: this one, D-ANUN, was the first. It was sold to British Midland in 1974 as G-BAPF after serving with Nora Air Services, Kassel.

Like Lufthansa, Condor eventually replaced its Viscounts with Boeing 737s transferred from the parent company. They featured a highly-polished natural metal fuselage with flying surfaces in yellow. This is 737-230 D-ABFT: this variant could accommodate 125 passengers in Condor service.

Condor also operated Boeing 727-200s. By the early 1990s, these and Lufthansa 727s had been replaced by Airbuses and D-ABKK illustrated had its registration reallocated to a Boeing 737-430 operated as Lufthansa Express.

Delivered to Lufthansa in 1979, Airbus A300B-4 D-AIBF *Kronberg-im-Taunus* was later used by Condor for a time and is seen at Frankfurt in what appears to be an interim colour scheme with a white fuselage top.

Condor's most modern type is the Airbus A320-212 and D-AICA is the first of eight, D-AICA to 'ICH, wearing registrations once worn by Lufthansa A310s. The smart colour scheme features a white fuselage top, wings and tailplane, with yellow lower fuselage, engines, fin and rudder. The first three entered service from April 1998, based at Berlin-Schönefeld.

Condor received its second McDonnell Douglas DC-10 D-ADQO in late 1979 and it entered service at the beginning of 1980. Engines were General Electric CF6-50s which burned about 6% less fuel than Lufthansa's DC-10s, causing the latter to be refitted with the later model engine.

The ideal choice for Condor's inclusive tour market was the Boeing 757-200: eighteen were delivered over four years from March 1990. At Frankfurt in April 1993 was D-ABNL, right in the middle of deliveries, having arrived in March 1992. It is being hauled by a German Cargo tug past the jet blast barriers to a departure gate.

The first of nine Boeing 767-300s was delivered to Condor at the end of July 1991. Registered D-ABUZ it is seen at Frankfurt in April 1993. It was followed by others from D-ABUA onwards and all had been received by mid-January 1995. In the centre background the Viscount used by Lufthansa for cabin training is just visible.

Something of a rarity, Condor's fourth Boeing 767-300 D-ABUC in June 1995 at Frankfurt in full Lufthansa colours. It was used by the latter for several months on a service to Sydney before reverting to Condor colours.

German regional carrier DLT's six HS.748s delivered between 1981 and 1984 operated a number of flights for Lufthansa which owned 26% of the company at that time and later took it over as Lufthansa CityLine. The HS.748s were retired as Fokker 50s became available, the last going in 1992.

Fokker 50s began to replace DLT's HS.748s in 1987 and D-AFKA was delivered on 7 August. Around thirty were received, but numbers began to decline as the Canadair RJ deliveries began in October 1992, the new jet having the same passenger capacity as the turboprop Fokker. A few of the latter remain in service with other operators, operating an occasional service for Lufthansa CityLine.

Contactair, with five de Havilland Canada (now Bombardier) Dash 8-311s, operated some services for CityLine. This is their last aircraft delivered, D-BKIM, at the manufacturer's Toronto-Downsview factory just prior to delivery in March 1993. Like the Fokker 50, the Dash 8s left Lufthansa service in 1996.

Lufthansa CityLine currently operates the forty-eight-seat Canadair RJ (also now Bombardier) and the eighty-seat Avro RJ85 (lower). The Canadair deliveries began in October 1992 and thirty-one were in service by mid-1999. The Avro RJ, a development of the BAe 146 with upgraded engines and instrumentation, entered service in 1997 and eighteen are used on European routes. Both types are luxuriously equipped with leather seating.

Deutsche Lufthansa Berlin-Stifftung (DLBS) restored this Arado Ar 79B in 1996 in a joint venture with its owners, the Museum für Verkehr und Technik (MVT), in Berlin. A former Luftwaffe aircraft, it was used in the Saar as SL-AAP for several years before becoming D-ECUV. It is now D-EMVT, reflecting its owners' initials, and it will return to the Museum for static exhibition in 2000, its flying days over.

First flown at Regensburg on 1 June 1940, this Messerschmitt Bf 108B-1 served with the Luftwaffe and was captured in Tunisia by US forces in May 1943. Shipped to the USA, it became NX54208, passing through several owners and, in 1985, became N108HP. Sold to Lufthansa in 1990 it was airfreighted to Frankfurt and restored, initially marked D-ELLI in memory of aviatrix Elli Beinhorn. Those marks were already officially used by a Cessna, so it became D-EBEI and was christened by Elli on 27 May 1993.